I told you everything
Jo Morris Dixon

VERVE
POETRY PRESS
BIRMINGHAM

PUBLISHED BY VERVE POETRY PRESS
https://vervepoetrypress.com
mail@vervepoetrypress.com

All rights reserved
© 2021 Jo Morris Dixon

The right of Jo Morris Dixon to be identified as author of this work has been asserted in accordance with section 77 of the Copyright, Designs and Patents Act 1988.

No part of this work may be reproduced, stored or transmitted in any form or by any means, graphic, electronic, recorded or mechanical, without the prior written permission of the publisher.

FIRST PUBLISHED OCTOBER 2021

Printed and bound in the UK
by Positive Print, Birmingham

ISBN: 978-1-912565-66-5

Cover Art Credit: Jo Morris Dixon

CONTENTS

helpline	7
Golden Shovel	8
constellation	9
period pad	10
resistance	11
The Prospective House Buyers	12
bleach	13
cat's ashes	14
6pm	15
Airbnb	17
Visitor Host (I)	18
Girl Guides	19
verisimilitude	20
tissue box	21
Visitor Host (II)	23
tuna melt	24
resistant materials	25
2004	26
mummy's sonnet	27

alliance	28
silence	30
Existential Heart on Skype	31

Acknowledgements

I told you everything

Before you know what kindness really is
you must lose things

Naomi Shihab Nye

helpline

you phoned the helpline at fourteen
hundred hours the croissant you had bought
in the morning now cold in your bag
the shop assistant wondered about you
in your ski jacket on such a sunny day

you phoned the helpline at fifteen
hundred hours the dishwasher was full
of bacteria growing on utensils
the girl who punched you at school was laughing
but stopped for a moment to bite her nails

you phoned the helpline at sixteen
hundred hours the tap in the kitchen had been
dripping in a way which made you think about music
the lifeguard in your local pool was looking for you
to check that you weren't holding your breath

you phoned the helpline at seventeen
hundred hours your period pad was wet and heavy
the teacher who had told you off for going into
the girls' toilets was shouting at her daughter
for not liking her prom dress

you phoned the helpline at eighteen
hundred hours the voice which answered waited for you
to speak before asking if you were in a safe space
the man who had hurt you opened his beer with his teeth
because there was no one to tell him not to

Golden Shovel

you sit there next to your English teacher and she tells you to take
your time and you think about counting bars of rest with him
and you can feel his hand placed on your knee in his room and
it makes you think about your arms and how you know each cut
well enough to draw them from memory and you worry about him
but the policewoman doesn't seem to care and it's so sunny out-
side even your mum was in a good mood when you went out in
shorts and unbrushed hair to make a statement and you cry a little
like you did the last time you sang in church choir and it makes stars
seem only good for writing about in sonnets destined for the bin and
you notice the height of the ceiling for the first time just like when he
looked at you afterwards and you wrote in your diary how no one will
ever believe you if you say something so you think about how to make
it all normal but now you are in the interview room listening to the
sound of a cheap plastic cup split in your fist and you want to lie face
down but you stare straight at the windows which have bars made of
brass except you can't play them and you don't want to go to heaven
if it means seeing euphoniums and trombones but your breathing is so
shallow that your English teacher has to tell you that you'll be fine

constellation

I could never remember the word
consolation so I thought of constellation
I used to love that expression
if it's any consolation
because it was the best hiding place
when everyone kept asking difficult questions
like how I was feeling
if I had been sleeping well
if I was going to orchestra on Saturday
I would just say *if it's any consolation*
I'm not like her
I'm not in hospital
I'm still coming to school

period pad

torn open to see what lies
under the first layer water-
colour crimson-lake cotton
wool summer-fruit-red even
in winter I was always curious
under the shower head watching
the blood clots remembering what
my best friend told me as a matter of
urgency as the boys at school were
learning about wet dreams we
were passing around pads

resistance

I'm sorry I have nothing to say
it's freezing outside, isn't it

yesterday I felt devastated about
can I have a glass of water

I'm sorry this is all about me
I like the plants in this room

I worry about birthdays
it's getting dark outside

remember when I fell through ice
I don't know how you do your job

I want to cry for fifty minutes
will you be here next week

my vagina doesn't feel right
there's not enough time left

I often like looking at my wrists
how are you going to get home

The Prospective House Buyers

The prospective house buyers looked at your unmade bed:
an unintentional homage to Tracy Emin. They didn't know
that the police had spoken to you whilst you were under
your duvet so your mum couldn't hear you from her attic
where she lay in bed even when the skies were baby blue.
They didn't know that you had already written elegies in
preparation for when everyone dies. They didn't know
that most nights you listened to your sister's breathing.
A minor achievement: to stay alive and keep dreaming.

bleach

you remember sitting / in your grandparents' kitchen / cold floor / dirty because of their old age lethargy / you can't picture what your little sister was wearing / but she trusted you / upper lip smile / drinking household bleach / utterly harmless / if only she had passed it on / to her imaginary friend / you remember sitting / in your grandparents' kitchen / everything wet and loud / colourful in a bad way / just before you arrived at the hospital / your only sister in a room with a fire / exit sign / to keep her safe / lying contorted on a bumpy bed / a toy from the Rice Krispies box in your hand / it was her turn to have it / you thought it might make her smile / a terrible consolation / you remember sitting / in your grandparents' kitchen / listening to your sister stop laughing / you tried shouting but the grownups were having fun / finally you left your sister / hoping her imaginary friend would look after her / you remember sitting / in your grandparents' kitchen / trying to focus / on the ticking clock / waiting for your sister / to get up

cat's ashes

today my sister passed me the only urn
we have kept in our house and cried
asking me whether I felt closer to our dead family
rescue cat or further away
given that Jack was never a cat like the ones you can find
on YouTube who like to fit into small spaces

6pm

I told you
I didn't feel
myself
I told you
as we walked
past the meat
counter to
choose cat
food for cats
with problems
like ours
I told you
my friend
has a therapist
who listens
to them at 6pm
every Tuesday
I told you
I was more
than sad
when you
found me
in bed still
on a Friday
after school
I told you
every time
I told you
how much

I hated it
when you
cooked
without salt
I told you
everything

Airbnb

there is nothing on the table
are slowly brightening
but the key is still in the lock
the itch on your back
your fists clenched
on top of it
and it's deep
a long time to work out
there are close-ups of sky-
the ceiling would
if it were painted cream
to the Airbnb
a swimming pool
at one another
your vibrator
since you last had sex
the curtains and
about things being open
spit with one eye closed
blood than before
take your red poppy off
the blue line
you move to sit
tie your laces tighter
your SIM card
you book a train ticket
Mount Fuji in its

the fluorescent lights
you should shut the door
you can't reach
you drink cold tea with
the toilet has a sink
the bath is dirty-white
you will need
how to turn the heater on
scrapers on the wall
still be too low
on the way
you imagine
two white cats staring
you've forgotten to pack
it's been too long
you don't shut
have dreams
you floss your teeth
make sure there's less
you think you should
you sit on the metro and ride
there's someone crying
next to them
you try to snap
no one is looking
which will frame
left side windows

Visitor Host (I)

make sure the lights are turned on / that the door is closed behind you / open the door just to make sure / you didn't switch anything off / that shouldn't be switched off / open the door again / close the door and walk away / do not turn around to look / at the door / walk towards the North Hall / balcony fire exit / remember to check / to see if anything unusual is happening / or has happened already / for example / can you smell gas / have the taxidermied animals been stolen / once you get there / radio security / tell them you are going / to open the fire exit / check for hazards / make sure the fire / exit door is firmly closed / walk to the entrance of the North Hall / wait for visitors to arrive / think about the fire / evacuation procedures / about the dirty switches / drink from your reusable water bottle / make sure you look presentable / think of what could possibly go wrong / say good morning / tell everyone about the walrus

Girl Guides

we met on a Girl Guides trip (she texted first)
which caused me to check my phone
in French class at school, a different school
to the one she was at which had a pool
but wasn't private she told me
to focus on the sound of leaves
crunching under my shoes whenever
I felt sad and that the dress code for
her fourteenth birthday party was red
which meant I expected her to invite me
so when she posted photos of herself
and her friends with Smirnoff Ice on MySpace
that night I hid my red turtleneck jumper
down the side of my bed and dreamt
about her saying sorry and kissing me
in a way which made me wake up
shocked to see that she had texted to say
my friend told me you like me, is it true?

verisimilitude

if you came back to Earth
as a spider I would make
sure not to kill you I would
bring you to the people who
scared you the most so you
could do the same to them
but this time as a spider
archetypal revenge with
me by your side feeding
you organic flies looking
after you until it's time
I know this makes sense
you have seen enough
clients like me but I have
never met anyone like you

tissue box

before you
leant over
to pick up
your glass
I thought
you were
going to
take a tissue
from the box
covered in
butterflies
the one
creature
I admitted
I didn't like
which made
me think of
a dream
where you
carried me
wrapped
in tissues
and left
me in
an empty
swimming
pool like an
unfinished
Hockney

painting
your clichéd
6pm client

Visitor Host (II)

You arrive at the Gallery Square Toilets and check for hazards. You try the accessible toilet but there is someone inside. You walk towards the women's toilets. You open the door and avoid eye contact. You hear a child ask *why is there a man in here?* Your chest feels tight as you walk into a cubical as quickly as you can. You look at the toilet seat, but you don't sit because that feels wrong. You're scared to leave the cubical in case the child is still there. You hear more children enter. It must be a school group. Someone tries to radio you and you realise you have no choice but to wash your hands and leave. You do this as the children stare. You exit feeling like you have a lifetime of school to get through.

tuna melt

the first time it happened felt warm then cold then terrifying
the chair you were sitting on in Religious Education was pale
grey next to a boy who wrote G-A-Y on your school planner

in his best bubble writing as you were handing out Bibles
at the beginning of class before your period had flooded
your pad and oozed through your two pairs of knickers

and thick boys' school trousers from M&S onto the seat
as the bell rang the boy stared at you and asked if you
had tuna sandwiches in your bag because you smelt

like fish and you lied and said *yes, a tuna melt from the
canteen* a terrible lie especially because you had given a
speech on animal rights in English just the week before

resistant materials

it's hard to forget when Lucy
saw your obvious period stain
on your Resistant Materials folder
which you had been sitting on
during the last lesson of the day
at school and you whispered
paint so she gave you the choice
of either a nighttime pad with wings
or a super tampon from her blazer
zipped pocket but you said it was *paint*
again which made you feel terrible
since you hated lying especially
to Lucy who had been off school
put on anti-depressants
given ten sessions in a room
only to return to your stained
folder and your lies

2004

I hadn't heard of Section 28 and how it was repealed in November 2003 in England and Wales but I knew that taking out the library's only copy of *Oranges Are Not the Only Fruit* would be difficult, so I tried to read as much of the book as I could behind *Harry Potter and the Chamber of Secrets* till the librarian asked what I was reading and said *do your parents know,* which made me turn the colour of my school tie. The librarian smiled like people do in films before the scene changes to a moody shot of the protagonist by the sea on a stormy day contemplating whether to swim in the tidal pool full of seaweed with no lifeguard on duty and said *you're reading a book from the Adult Section,* at which point the babies who were normally crying stopped and I thought about the Childline poster at school which now had the word GAY graffitied across the boy on the phone looking sort of sad with the number 0800 1111 printed in one of those typefaces that tried too hard to be popular with teenagers and I thought about everything I'd say if I called up but as the librarian asked me again to put *Oranges* back on the shelf even Childline didn't comfort me much as I realised the counsellor could be someone like her

mummy's sonnet

she weighed the butter and sugar
even though she should have been able to do it by eye
turned on the blender and mixed butter into sugar
she most likely let out a sigh as she crouched down
to get the flour from the bottom cupboard
she was probably cracking eggs into her mixture
before adding the flour in small, measured amounts
deciding on what food colouring to add to the icing
she might have smiled when she told my sister
that the fairy cakes were ready to be decorated
when I sat in the police station to give my statement
after the police had left our living room, she said
If I had known about all of this I wouldn't
have spent the morning making fairy cakes

alliance

drinking out
of a glass
my therapist
washed
without
a dishcloth
something
she neglected
to dry
guessing
how many
seconds
we might
sit in
precarious
silence
daring her
to comment
on my minty
breath my new
hairstyle
my long
sleeves
in summer
if she let me
I would buy
her a watch
be there
when she

taps herself
in and out
of the tube
help her find
matching socks
make sure
Tinder is
installed on
her phone
after all
I found her
online
inside her
rented room
I want her
to tell me
how I'm
the best
client she's
ever had

silence

the last time I carried the blue choir benches
was one of the first times I felt myself
in a way which made me
remember that time in spring
when I realised Gram was Father
Christmas and even though I loved her
she would die soon so I stayed awake
on Christmas Eve and saw Gram turn
into a memory that I'll always think about
when asked in therapy how it feels
to sit in a silence which I used to call prayer

Existential Heart on Skype

I still remember the last time I saw my therapist
it was dark outside because it was 18:50, London

March 2020, and we had smiled at the beginning
about how she had put a single square of tissue

underneath her glass and mine and when it felt
like we were laughing too much I told her how

the virus was everywhere, just like sadness
and asked whether she could really trust me

not to have it or her other clients for that matter
this was back when the general view in the UK

was that only people who had travelled from certain
countries on PHE's list might have it and she told me

that she trusted her clients and I told her how angry
I felt that one time she left her used balls of tissue in

front of the water jug we were meant to be sharing
how I suspected she had not gotten the flu jab which

was why she had missed our last session of 2019 and told
her she probably would have been hit by a car if it weren't

for me telling her that she needed better reflective clothing
she agreed we should meet online from next week instead

I gestured at her plants, so she promised she'd have a plant
in her Skype background as well as a bookshelf and part of

a curtain which was navy blue just so I'd know what to expect
I told her that I probably wouldn't see her in person for years

so when I checked her website to see if she had changed her
location or prices I was disturbed to see no updates despite

lockdown which led to us falling out but we're still speaking
and I have resisted sending her an existential heart on Skype

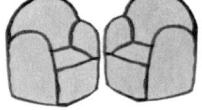

ABOUT THE AUTHOR

Jo Morris Dixon grew up in Birmingham and now lives in London. Her poetry has been published in *The Poetry Review, Poetry Wales, Ambit Magazine, Oxford Poetry* and *The Signal House Edition*. She was longlisted for the 2015 Plough Poetry Prize and the 2019 and 2020 National Poetry Competition. *I told you everything* is her debut pamphlet.

ACKNOWLEDGEMENTS

Thank you to the editors at *The Poetry Review, Poetry Wales, Ambit Magazine, Oxford Poetry* and *The Signal House Edition* for publishing my poems. Thank you to all the judges who longlisted my work for the 2015 Plough Poetry Prize and the 2019 and 2020 National Poetry Competition.

Epigraph is taken from Naomi Shihab Nye's poem, 'Kindness', in *Words Under the Words: Selected Poems* (Eighth Mountain Press, 1994). 'Golden Shovel' takes its ending words from William Shakespeare's *Romeo and Juliet*.

Many thanks to Stuart Bartholomew at Verve Poetry Press for publishing my debut pamphlet. Thank you also to my poetry mentors, especially Jacqueline Saphra and Richard Scott, who taught me at the Poetry School and Faber Academy respectively.

Thank you to my partner, Mary Jean, who helped me believe in myself and my poetry. Finally, my heartfelt thanks to my family, friends and all the people who have ever looked after me.

ABOUT VERVE POETRY PRESS

Verve Poetry Press is a quite new and already award-winning press that focussed initially on meeting a local need in Birmingham - a need for the vibrant poetry scene here in Brum to find a way to present itself to the poetry world via publication. Co-founded by Stuart Bartholomew and Amerah Saleh, it now publishes poets from all corners of the UK and beyond - poets that speak to the city's varied and energetic qualities and will contribute to its many poetic stories.

Added to this is a colourful pamphlet series, many featuring poets who have performed at our sister festival - and a poetry show series which captures the magic of longer poetry performance pieces by festival alumni such as Polarbear, Matt Abbott and Genevieve Carver.

The press has been voted Most Innovative Publisher at the Saboteur Awards, and has won the Publisher's Award for Poetry Pamphlets at the Michael Marks Awards.

Like the festival, we strive to think about poetry in inclusive ways and embrace the multiplicity of approaches towards this glorious art.

https://vervepoetrypress.com
@VervePoetryPres
mail@vervepoetrypress.com